T0114955

SEASON OF SHADOWS
Poems

John Ngong Kum Ngong

Langaa Research & Publishing CIG
Mankon, Bamenda

Publisher
Langaa RPCIG
Langaa Research & Publishing Common Initiative Group
P.O. Box 902 Mankon,
Bamenda
North West Region
Cameroon
Langaagrp@gmail.com
www.langaa-rpcig.net

Distributed in and outside N. America by African Books Collective
orders@africanbookscollective.com
www.africanbookscollective.com

ISBN-10: 9956-550-52-3

ISBN-13: 978-9956-550-52-4

© John Ngong Kum Ngong 2019

Table of Contents

Foreword

It is on record that Africa is the highest continent in the contemporary world bedevilled by a plethora of socio-political, economic, and cultural dilemmas such as corruption, state-repression, ethnocentric rivalry, civil wars, economic sloppiness, cultural malaise, moral decadence, and neo-colonialism. In fact, these ills have made the continent the laughing stock of the world, pushing her to a subaltern position in global politics and diplomacy. In the midst of this cacophony and dystopia, many African writers have not been indifferent. As the biblical prophets in the Old Testament, they have dedicated their art to the service of their community by highlighting the socio-political and economic lop-sidedness in contemporary Africa and by cautioning the citizens and the post-colonial African political elites of the Armageddon that will befall them if things do not change for the better. Any post-colonial African writer who, somehow, shuns this call of naming and shaming is akin to the elder in the story who sat comfortably and watched the she-goat suffer and die from the pains of parturition on its tether. As it were, the general understanding is that the time has come when the African writer should have the temerity to salvage what could still be salvaged from the recurrent cycle of post-colonial stupidity and visionlessness.

The Anglophone Cameroonian poet, John Ngong Kum Ngong, in his poetry collection, entitled *Season of Shadows*, has demonstrated that any African writer who is insensitive in articulating the plight and miasma of despair of the downtrodden African masses will sooner or later, by an inexorable law of nature, become irrelevant since in Africa, the functionality of art and its aesthetic virility are inseparable. In other words, the African writer does not only see himself as an entertainer but also as the gadfly of his society who cannot be silent in the face of excruciating injustice against his people. Thus, Ngong Kum Ngong's *Season of Shadows* is a collection of forty-three poems that articulate thematic discourses in post-colonial Africa such as political power, corruption, ethnicity, individualism, repression, nationalism, cultural imperialism, national fragmentation, and above all, the tragic failure of leadership. These ills are appropriately expressed in the collection in order to conscientise the African against such post-colonial infirmities. In this connection, the title of the collection is metaphorically apt because it conveys a society that is ridden with confusion and collective obscurity, that is, a society which is going through a "season of shadows"! This title, therefore, gives an image of what the poems in the collection are all about.

In "Season of Shadows", the title poem, the poet-persona brings out the trauma and distress of the post-colonial citizen caused by the oppressive machinery in which he finds himself. The speaker, in the poem, addresses a maid "rammed with burns and boils" during "this season of shadows" and comforts her that "the new moon will come up" to change her condition. The poet, further, criticises the repressive post-colonial machinery for subjugating "peaceful minds" and "noble hearts" who are committed to seeing things work in their society. This thematic discourse also finds in-roads in "No Right to Favour" where the speaker is addressing post-colonial leaders, and their lackeys, about their corrupt and irresponsible leadership. According to the speaker, these leaders "have no right to favour/for the trade of truth for francs and "for the racket in your blood" (17). The poet-persona, therefore, paints an atmosphere of distrust and gloom in the postcolony – an atmosphere which is also highlighted in

"Shameless Shadows", "Sententious Shadows", "Stubborn Spirit", and "Intellectual Shadows" where the poet handles issues of post-colonial betrayal, anger, dystopia, and confusion and paints a society where its inhabitants are full of atrocities, hatred and evil machinations.

John Ngong Kum Ngong also handles discursive issues of political hypocrisy, deception, ethnocentric consciousness, and greed in the contemporary context. His ideological consciousness is erected on the platform that the postcolonial nation cannot be constructed on the foundation of a tribal idiom and naïve citizens who are prepared to sway to any form of unfounded promises. In "Harrowing Moments", the poet chastises the ideology of tribalism in contemporary Africa – an ideology that has fragmented most African nations, rendering them vulnerable and susceptible to ethnic tension and conflict. In this context of ethnic exclusionism, the poet subpoenas the segregated people in "We Belong" to assert themselves in their society and "show the world that we belong" because, as he says, "We are part of this nation." In "Baseless Promises", equally, the persona criticises the credulous and gullible post-colonial citizens who are easy victims of the political cants of post-colonial politicians. He argues that "Baseless promises ruin a nation" and "stunt a people" and lampoons the post-colonial masses who continuously fall prey to the perfidy and duplicity of these politicians. In the midst of all these ills, the poetic 'I' also laments in "When Innocence is Slain" how his countrymen are suffering in the hands of perfidious and greedy political leaders in their society. The speaker tells his countrymen and brethren that "The beast in the heart of greed/the shine of all that is dung/and the lust so strong in men/make my head spine round and round/like a dead leaf from a branch" (37).

Furthermore, the discursive contents of social justice and human rights are also the levers of Ngong Kum Ngong's poetic consciousness. The poet believes that the construction of a postcolonial nationhood is impossible when injustice and the blatant abuse of human rights are the political cultures in the postcolony. Thus, in some of his poetic renditions in this collection, he sounds his trumpet-call and rallies the people for social change. In "You Dare Not Be Silent", the persona urges the post-colonial masses not to be silent in the face of unbearable social injustice, human rights abuse, and disorder in their society, by boldly declaring that "Patriots dare not be silent/when fifth columns grow violent/and our dignity drops tears" (46). In this guise, a stinging critique of post-colonial subjects who remain silent in the face of injustice and oppression is here offered, for, as Archbishop Desmond Tutu argues, anyone who refuses to speak against injustice and oppression in his society is in a way supporting those who are guilty of these ills. The poet's revolutionary discourse is also ingrained in "Still My Heart" where he invites his countrymen to stand up against "beasts bleeding the nation dry" (49). In fact, from the perspective of Marxist discourse, the poet subscribes to the Marxist idiom that the philosopher has described and explained the world and the only task now is to change it.

"Remember the Broken Fences" discusses issues of nationalism and nation-building which, in post-colonial Africa, can only be achieved through respecting human rights, freedoms, and social justice. Furthermore, the poet's revolutionary vision is ingrained in "Special Call" and "Dig Deep Deep Down". In the former, the masses are exhorted to harken to the "special call" of freedom and liberty and transform their society from its present dystopian nature to an oasis of justice and equality. The speaker says that "There is no reason mates/to think we cannot stand/the hawks oppressing minds/not glad to lose their butter" (15). "Dig Deep Down" follows up on this by a didactic call to the youths to be implicated in social transformation in their society by going "beyond the swamp land/ also deeded to us all/ to find the key to victory/ with eyes of gleaming resolve" (16). The poetic 'I' instils confidence in the younger generation to assert themselves in the fatherland and not to allow pretentious political big-wigs to trample on them because "The land was deeded to us/to dig deep down to survive" (16). In a prophetic tone, the poet-persona warns post-colonial leaders, in "When Time Will Rule", that they should reconcile with the masses before nemesis and retributive justice catches up with them.

The poet reveals himself in this collection as one with unshakable radical humanism; a poet for the downtrodden who is religiously concerned about their existential conditions. In "Likely Tempest", the poverty-stricken conditions of children in the postcolony call for lament through a graphic style captured through vivid description and metaphors where "naked children with dry mouths/gaze in fear a likely tempest" (47). This imagistic language depicts the extent of wretched poverty in the speaker's immediate social context and the entire postcolonial world. The speaker's ethical humanism continuously pushes him to fight against these socio-political structures and forces that are responsible for the plight and destitution of these masses, laying bare his despair: "Sometimes my rage reddens unchecked" (47). The same humanistic consciousness is articulated in "Left in the Cold" where the poet chastises those who preach tribal hatred in their society "that could beget a bloodbath" (40). The poet, further, laments the naivety of the postcolonial youth who can afford to sacrifice their lives "for hoggish statesmen to rule/prying open thighs to live/unaffected, remorseless/even this season of tears" (40). In other words, the poet is cautioning the young generation not to be swayed by the rhetoric of post-colonial politicians whose vaulting ambitions have nothing to do with alleviating their existential needs.

Finally, the poet, John Ngong Kum Ngong, assures the citizens of the postcolony that behind every dark cloud there is a silver lining. He comforts the masses that even in the present and recurrent cycle of despair, caused by this "season of shadows", in their various societies, there is a glimmer of hope in the horizon. In "Burn Your Rags", there is the hope that despite the present political mayhem, no-one should recline or sink into desperation because that darkest time of the night is at dawn. The masses are thus enjoined to be courageous in the face of oppression and hardship because it is "When the heart is filled with grief/when our birthright stands in the cold/ and vultures step in to sing" that "the owner of the world meets us/gives us words and material/to break the barriers round us/and hoist the flag of freedom/in a land that loves thraldom" (48).

Bate Besong, in an interview with Pierre Fandio says, inter alia, that "Art provides the writer the arena in which to explore political ideas as refracted through human character" since "Literature deals with human beings and their relationships over time in space". This argument filters through the creative consciousness of John Ngong Kum Ngong because *Season of Shadows* can be rightfully described as a critical and acerbic diagnosis of the socio-political situation in postcolonial Africa. In fact, this poet can be considered the unacknowledged legislator of his society! The poems, in this eleventh collection, are deceptively simple, aesthetically complex, and ideologically intriguing because the poet wraps his message in a plethora of literary devices such as paradox, suspense, metaphors, allusions, personification, irony, satire, humour, and contrast.

The poems, in this collection, therefore, are not only politically 'correct' but also artistically profound!

Zuhmboshi Eric Nsuh, PhD
Lecturer, Literary Critic, and Political Analyst

Shameless Shadows

This is no season to be born;
no season to trust your own wits,
with shadows for next door neighbours
and dogs sniffing the air to warn
that man runs the risk of dying
cold in the chilly hands of Hate.
This is no season to be born.

Shadows are companions I dread
like the merciless edge of hate
with peppers and nefarious plots.
I ache in bone flesh and spirit
in a land in the crushing grip
and grinding boots of bad spearheads,
shameless shadows in search of prey.

This is no time to be silent
with siblings at each other's throat
and men and women slashing Love
in a land lit with wickedness.
This cuts the heart out of my dream
of a steady state bright with stars.
Shameless shadows beside the stream
and houses that house poverty
celebrate the death of freedom.

Sententious Shadows

They follow you everywhere,
shadows without your consent
thin like sandy pumpkin leaves,
their misty minds in their mouths
ready always to call you
for a feast at witching time.

This is their optimum time.
You dare not dare their forethoughts
as they push their way with you
through rough and twisted terrain
unseen, holding fresh flowers
to lure you away from light.

They come to the fore sometimes
to your shame and discontent
dry and sooty like charcoal,
their liquid hearts in their eyes
ready always to pull you
back from the path of justice.
This is their spawning season.
We need to walk out on them
for their seeds to bite the dust.
They are false and sententious,
living within call of dust
so take heed lest you lose face.

Intellectual Shadows

The wind is on holiday,
dragon flies purr with pleasure
in the shadow of palm trees.
Their slim shadows this season
beat their wings in merriment
under the shade of my person.

Nothing has in essence changed
since the wind, less passionate
this particular time off,
refuses to shake fruit trees.
This is a hairy season
when the beast in man rises
and plagues mankind day and night,
choking with hate innocence.

Intellectual shadows howl
but unlike the wind, they bend
when the god of the stomach
bids them burn their crowns for crumbs.
Their shadows they misconceive
for the light of leadership.
It is time that this season
I faced my shadow with nerve
or like a slave for keeps, bow
in the shadow of shadows.

Shifty Shadow

Sometimes it falls behind
thinking of its master
whose heart heaves half-naked,
hoping to have new clothes.
Sometimes it runs ahead
casting Delphic darkness
on the issues of the day,
shifty shadow unabashed.

The shadow of the past limps
haggard, into my bedroom
threatening to smash my head.
Scared stiff, I jump out of bed
struggling to hide my anger
in the soot of yesterday
and the cold feet of today.

I hope I will no more sigh
when the wind returns from leave
and shadows glide into holes
painted with colours of change.
I hope to see the sun rise
from the ashes of our lives
even when dull cowardice
casts a shadow this season.

Silly Season

The shadow of the cypress tree
I see this season of shadows,
beside the begrimed shallow stream
flowing grudgingly down the dell
near where displaced souls have settled
this season of dark hidden ends,
reminds me of your faint shadow
passing before me every day,
calling to mind cruel deception.
You do everything to conceal
the heart of your aspirations
yet I still long to embrace it.

You have betrayed my love my heart
but I am still attached to you
even in the darkest darkness.
I do really feel your presence
this silly season of shadows
taking away in pitch darkness
the credulity of my love.
I dare not dare you daft shadow
this troubling season of shadows,
teeth sunk deep in my scanty flesh.
The darkness of my own shadow
recalls the failure to face self.

Season Of Shadows

My heart goes out to you
maid, rammed with burns and boils
this season of shadows.
After the seduction,
the rape and the stonewall,
song and dance went downhill.

My heart beats for you still
deep in the heart of fray
this season of black clouds.
Torn away from your roots
the source of your strength miss,
love and peace cut and run.

For the hills I head prey
fraught with spleen and slow burns
this season of shadows.
Sore and left in the lurch
the new moon will come up
before the earth grabs me.
Why should I not be mad
this season of madness?
Peaceful minds have been irked,
noble hearts coaxed to kill
this season of bad blood.
Scorpions breed in my head.

Stubborn Spirit

I refuse to accept
you feel no cold comfort
this season of billows.
Your fondness for frankness
flows more or less inward
this season of suspense.
Maybe I am moonstruck
not to keep on fanning
the fervid flame of love
lit in my breast years back.

I refuse to accept
you are a turnabout
this season of bad blood.
Your figure is cut straight
to fit in with the storm
howling outside, flaring
in the heart of our love.
How can you be so cold
at this stage of slaughter?
I refuse to accept
you feel no deflation
this season of rancour.
The shadows on the wall
close to your heart have teeth.

Baseless Promises

Promises without footing cease not
since this season of shadows started.
Everything around is vinegary
and the wind is blowing recklessly.
Being so gullible, you have not known
the wickedness of the just arrived
in the cathedral of arrivistes,
nor the arrogance of parvenus.
Maybe this implacable season
would extirpate the scales from your eyes
and put a stone lid on betrayal.
Baseless promises ruin a nation.

Roam no more around the embankment
briber and the bribed have erected
overnight despite the sea's protest.
In a twinkling they have also raised
a castle in which to cast bright minds.
I warned you many, many years back
but being naïve you did not listen.
You took me for an adversary then
even when the stars reasoned with you.
Maybe this discomfiting season
we would start speaking the same language
in the bosom of the friendly moon.
Baseless promises stunt a people.

Note To An Artist

When, when but this season
have bigotry and greed
overflowed their gnarled banks,
determined without masks
to shake hands with Iagos
and drown all left-wingers?

I will never give tongue
in praise of reckless tongues.
They wreak havoc always
on their suborned way up.
Once they get to the top,
pandemonium breaks loose.
Were it not that the heart
at the thought of my roots
and the cry of orphans
left a note on my desk,
wanton tongues should be shot,
bigotry and greed lynched.

Now that we sleep awake
this season of stupor
I will choose what we read,
where to go when leaves weep
in the heat of the sun
and who not to believe.

Harrowing Moments

I am sick of pleading with you
broken embittered heart on ash
to no longer curse the darkness
closing in on our bloated land,
enfolding shadows and phantoms.
Tribalism and hate have grown,
blunt minds advance, the sharp are smashed
increasing the blood in the streets.
Do something drastic like Brutus
lest your heart be given away.

I have found something outrageous
to ponder over this season.
Tribalism and hate break loose
under impudent, puerile heads
in the shadow of a smug god.
Gone are Um Nyobe's sun rays
and all the dreams and brilliant minds.
The frigid elegance of force
breeds rebellion and senseless war.
I am tired of watching lame,
mothers dropping their weeping tears
over scions not sure to survive
these harrowing moments of shame.

Weep Not Though

This is not the time to weep though
nor the station to spread your mat
and lie down lowly like a slave.
The daddy long legs that lived here
have all absconded to the bush
and the weaver birds have left too,
back to the palm trees we planted
before venturing to this place
glittering with gall and bad blood.

This is the season to shed sham
and wean the babies in your mind
from procrastination and fright
to win the manumission fight.
Why did you become such a snitch
for creatures who hate give and take
and gamble with our people's lives,
you who taught me how to strike out
against strong currents in mid stream?
Your decorum you still can stitch
and your reputation restore
this dawning of long-sightedness,
the season to stand up and speak
for beautiful lofty forethoughts
and the need of shedding all sham.

We Belong

Our navel strings fly the flag,
stung by the bee of hatred.
Stars have gathered in the square
to give meaning to our lives,
stand up to the terrorists
raising themselves to the sky,
to show the world we belong
my sore heart and embittered soul.

Our navel strings remember us
unsexed by the forces of greed.
They scream surrounded by snitchers
to call the attention of tongues,
pull down the halls of injustice
and write off the madness of hate
to mend the way to governance.
The earth testifies we belong.

Our navel strings dip the flag,
gathered in a large stadium
to kiss us back to our roots,
pluck the wings of oppression
and let the fingers of right
draw up a new legal code.
You cannot dare to stay back.
We are part of this nation.

Remembering Broken Fences

We are here to clear the pathway
and stand our ways in words this way.
We are not usurpers dear Earth
drinking the blood of young palm trees
to weave cobras round your bosom.
We are not shadows unnoticed.

We are here to school our children
to stand for the rights of others
and heal the wounds of those weeping.
We are neither mercenaries
nor hirelings with twisted speeches.
We are here to turn on the light.

We weep for what has been broken
and paint the foul face of terror
building boats to ferry weak souls
across the border of their loot.
We have no more words to employ
to mend our thoughts and reactions.
Let the fire in your fat eyes
and the arrows in your ego
make thicker the blood in your veins
as you come into the stadium
to remake or mar our history.
Remember the broken fences.

Special Call

In the belly of grief
beside a yawning hole
where for years we have toiled
and dreamt watching the sun
dress and undress each day
or fed our minds with sweets
from the masons of lies,
we scarcely kissed laughter
or felt the smooth touch of love.

Today a call comes home
from the depths of Memory
wrapped in expectations.
It is a special call
that must be answered now.
We should stand up and go
whether into darkness
or into bright daylight,
we must answer the call now.
Answer the call or rot
in the belly of grief.
There is no reason mates
to think we cannot stand
the hawks oppressing minds,
not glad to lose their butter.

Dig Deep Deep Down

It was deeded to us all
young man draped in starless robes,
the swamp land beneath the mount
teeming with shrimps and wildlife.
I think you have to dig deep
to find the key to your roots
rather than stick to juggling,
cleaning the bums of bumblers,
airheads still unmeet to beat
the flame ravishing our pride.
Sunk deep into corruption,
the ogres dressed in red suits
vow to cut down all rivals
to rise and embrace the stars.

You have to dig deep deep down
young man, beyond the swamp land
also deeded to us all
to find the key to victory
with eyes of gleaming resolve.
The land was deeded to us
who shout deep things everyday
to retrieve the key of truth
and keep awake drowsy heads.
The land was deeded to us
to dig deep down to survive.

No Right To Favour

Comparing you to a bat
is favour not merited.
A bat sees well in the night
and it is more temperate.
You see neither in the day
nor in shadiness and night.
Cowards tremble, idiots curb
and clap full blast when you speak.

Bizarre soul gone to the dogs,
inclement heart, razor tongue.
Comparing you to a bat
is favour not merited.
A bat feeds on mosquitoes
ready always to take off
when the seasons become harsh.
You feed on leaves of the heart
and ensnare your prey at night
to feed red meat to your kind.
You have no right to favour
for the trade of truth for francs.
You have no right to favour
for the racket in your blood.

Violence On The Pedestal

I know you can no longer wait
in this stuffiness and fever,
this scaring oppressive setting.
The heart for sure needs comfort first
then the freedom to leave the ground
and land on any beauteous bloom.
It is not the case in this place
in the need of a human face.

I know you have a mind to sing
against the tin gods of darkness
who for many, many years now
have had for tea the heart of love,
set violence on a pedestal
and my inquisitive eyes bleared
with brochures from the underworld.
Such menu enfeebles the soul.

Write whatever you want to write
against each and every bleared state
without breaking the wings of hope.
I will sing for hearts separated
in the mad war of primacy
and pierce through the profiles of folk
leading us without calibre
to the edge of a precipice.

Simple Song Writer

1

I am just a simple song writer,
my songs simple and fraternal.
I have been writing for long now
drawing tears and weeing myself
in the midst of Spartan writers
mute in this season of terror.

Tell me soulmate just what happened
when an angry wind blew this way.
What went wrong when we came of age
just when the sky was getting clear
and the Earth was preparing hard
to watch us beat our purple drums?

Did the wind break one of your wings
or blow down the trees in your head?
In any case I am the same,
just a simple writer dying
to paint the colours of our land
noticed annoyingly by none.

2

I am just a simple poet
with no garlands round my neck,
just a simple poet with eyes
that see even in darkness.
I eat the food peasants eat,

feel their emotions also
and paint sunrise and sunfall
from the cabin of my poems
with them daily, clothed in black.

I know you will laugh at me
and conclude I am a fool
bereft of a name worthy
yet I can laugh full throated
like an eagle on her eggs.
At least I am more human,
more thoughtful and more caring
than souls who force to be seen.
Do not let rage consume you.

I am just a simple poet,
a grain of sand in your rice,
just a simple poet with brains
to understand this queer world.
The nails of life also sink
deep into my hairless skin.

3
I do not sing for goats.
They eat up every leaf
and kill both stem and roots.
They cannot eat the weeds
creeping towards our homes.
They are such a nuisance,
making my pains grow worse.

I will not let them stop me
nor any shammer move me
to look away from the sun
though my weakness makes me faint.
I hope to pull through this life
no matter the vales and hills
for though lonely, God minds me.

I am a puny drummer
trying to beat your cold heart hot
this sad season of shadows.
I may get caught in the dark
getting ready a new beat
to bring joy to joyless hearts.
I will never sing for goats.

 4
I sing to ease my mind
in the mouth of grim thoughts,
when at the bend of the road
open wounds dance before me.

I sing to free my heart
in the hall of tension,
when in the heart of the night
monsters come to drain my dreams.

I sing to be myself
in the midst of clamour,
when at the crossroads of life
dubious souls stand in my way.

This red season of shadows
I sing to soothe your minds
and weave faith in your hearts
to carve anew our history.
We can take another path
this season of cruel shadows.
I sing to unlace our souls
fastened to the tree of lies.

5

These unhinged songs of mine I guess
will untie the cords in your heart
and redirect your way back home.
I believe not even the storm
nor the silenced voice of courage
will make you abandon the track
we took to build on this hard soil.

These unhinged songs of mine I think
will slaughter the fool in your blood
and open the door for your leave.
I am sure the handcuff of fear
and the yoke of your ignorance
will not blow out the light I see
burning bright untied, in your eyes.

Back home, remember not to bar
the mind that desires to blow
like the wind where it aspires.
I am only waiting for time
to stand in the entrance of Rule,

state my case before the key Judge
for all to see my cracked history.

 6
I burst into song often
to sing you to your senses
when sharp-tongued shadows turn in
and violent souls file their teeth
to pick through maiden marrow
searching for newly screened sap.

I set to music sometimes
the folly of hollow men
shadowing lean learned heads
drunk with arrogance and scorn.
I can hear your enraged heart
singing and cursing, worked up.

This season is a weird one
for in truth I get wind of
hooligan voices clapping,
moronic voices in song,
all of them on the alert
this season of shameless acts.
In annoying times like these
I seldom turn a blind eye
to Othello's tragic flaw.
Do not break ranks my people
even when sneer shadows scream.

A Penguin's Broodings

I cannot fly like an eagle,
my wings delicate and feeble.
I see other birds in my place
hopping around with confidence
and hawks scratch the land undisturbed.
I have no emotions to curb
in the face of rape and shooting.
I am not jealous of eagles
but when my kind is trampled on,
I hobble towards the wounded.

My weakness expects much from you.
I have a very short life span.
You have a better chance to live
even in the womb of the night.
A seemingly warm heart sights me
but I look away to the clouds
gathering in the horizon.
Is the friend really moved to tears?
I fear he may be a vulture
in the teeth of biting hunger.
Can my weakness crawl to your home
and be served a seat in your heart?
Can my siblings sit close to you
and be shown the way to laughter?

Ripe To Make The Difference

You are ripe to understand this.
The mind and heart do quarrel
every moment and anywhere
as long as blood pumps in their veins.
You are the mind, I am the heart
sailing across dangerous seas
to wear the green cap of my heart
on your bald and obstinate head.
You are ripe to make the difference.

If you think love is out of mind
I think words have driven you mad.
Where we come from near running streams
remember, waits for you and I,
hands lifted towards the heavens.
We are destined for each other
walking through darkness and fire
beyond this wasteland our graveyard.
You are ripe to understand this,
especially now when sadists
in the guise of liberators
comb the land for ill-gotten gains.

Keep The Stream Clean

The morbid murmur of the stream
creeping through the fog of our wits
reminds me of the cabal plays
staged through the darkness of midnight.
Pundits hustling for dubious posts,
inept at settling what they are
lend a hand to divert the stream.

With my strength bent, my will wilting
and my dreams stuttering in mud
like an orphan naked and dry,
the tearing murmur of the stream
crawling through our stone consciences
reminds me of the uphill task
before us like a colossus,
maintaining the course of the stream.

I wish I knew a shorter road
and the craft to carry us home
when the ruse of fools fails to work.
I speak not out of sympathy
to pick up crumbs under tables
standing in the heart of our dreams.
I speak wondering when we set out,
why we are still so divided
instead of keeping the stream clean.

Directionless Driver

The whisper of the wind
at the break of each day
delivers news that tenses.
More tongues have been sliced today
and rows of houses burnt down.
Trees with fruits bow in terror.

The whisper of the wind
at the break of each day
reminds me of your juggling.
The murmur of green sparrows
dies between your saw-like teeth.
Surreptitiously you feast
under chandeliers from France.

Dull directionless driver,
innocent souls have sunk
under your bleak direction.
Women cast their spent arms stunned,
calling all men to cross swords
with those daring their peace pact.
The last lingering furious flames
will not die out save you drop
dry directionless driver
on the payroll of pythons.

They Risked Their Lives

They risked their lives to unyoke us
but we have no regard for them.
Idiots have made donkeys of them
and I want to give myself up
driven to the verge of madness.
The nationalists were selfless,
with no faked patriotic chaplets
nor pseudo love in their language.

Red rogues branded them terrorists
but we have high regard for them.
The sun has not set them aside
nor the moon their endeavours mocked
to make us chortle with the world.
I blush to brush their dreams aside
cognizant of the blood they spilled
fighting for the cause of free rein.

Great patriots, we weep to fancy
you are not honoured by your own.
There is a song in my inside
that can only be put in words
when the light in the tunnel shines.
You risked your lives to rescue us
from the red deadly Octopus
out from the Atlantic Ocean.

What Matters Most

Whatever happened to the treaty
we signed when the sky was overcast
and our run down coast suffocating,
is second to the bleakness I see
carving and painting death everywhere
with material that will hardly fade.
Whatever happened to the pledges
we endorsed when the weather was foul
and the tongues of neighbours so caustic,
is second to the soreness I feel
watching my genus pass on so young,
freezing-dry the marrow in my bones.

What matters most these back-breaking days
under the weight of Frankenstein's load
is to stick to each other like glue.
Our lot has been that of non-persons
but our precepts we will not forsake
even under Dracula's agents.

I cannot count the atrocities
and the hands that scoop dust for powder.
For years we have gathered with hands tied
the legitimate tears of patriots.
Henceforth I offer them my backbone
the songs that have cured my blood pressure.

Genocide In Silence

Until monocracy drops
and the sun walks out on me,
I will continue to sing
the atrocities of sharks
and drum into your large ears
the genocide in our silence.
Together with fresh fighters,
we can leap from this ocean
like an incensed octopus
aggrieved by the sea bottom
and conquer new territory.
I choose not to stay tied up here.

Though monocrats have keen eyes
and know the right way to take,
though they go to bed armoured
and awake looking refreshed,
they tremble and do not see
the cutting light in front of them.

Whether their glory they drown
or nurture it day by day,
whether the cries of their kids
and the darkness of the sky
fed up with them multiply
or not, their requiem will be held.

Blunt Mind

You may be affixed in a rock,
you may kid around in witchcraft
with the leading light of darkness.
I am made of tempered fabric
yet I fight for what befits me.
I fight for a conflict-free world,
an understanding Africa
whittled by Africans themselves.

I resist outside management
wanting always its own system
and dry concepts in golden plates.
Our joy is enshrouded in tears,
the heart of our goodwill beats low
and the voice that becalmed us gone.
I was disposed to believe him,
Lumumba the visionary
till the pain in his mind accused,
plastering the door to self-rule.
See, the spirit of love still throbs
for the soul of my continent.
To whoever looks for our way
I present you this fresh flower,
the road to a better outlet
believing in ourselves not myths
stewed in the mess of red people.

Itching To Turn

The desire to turn
this season of treason
beckons like a hot kiss.
Questions upon questions
shroud reason without doubt.
What if darkness shines on
and the world refuses
to feel our agony?
I point my small finger
at the demons of self
bent on suicidal feats
in a land without feet.

The desire to turn
pants like a thirsty deer.
I see rivers of blood
flow down every pathway.
All night long hyenas howl
and the heart becomes cold,
as cold as frozen fish.
I have measured the urge,
wearied still by the blood
running down the pavements
in a land without lungs,
a land of hate and lust.

When Time Will Rule

In the folly of your heart
you mistake the land for yours
and think you are the saviour.
The magic carpets with which
you ensnare people like rats
will fly away when Time rules.

In the conceit of your heart
you feel you are the all and all
and mistake the people's calm
for love and satisfaction.
Your voice will be heard no more,
your power will be thrown out
like soiled water when Time rules.

Time is closing in on you
and all the magic lanterns
you use to blind the masses
will be blown out when Time rules.
You have fumbled for long now
boss but can turn from tumbling
if you cry with the people
and your heart goes out with them.

Not At Any Price

The mind claps in stupefaction
lying in the laps of the gods,
unaware we had trod this path
before the flame of affection
stopped burning in our people's hearts.

There is war in everyone's heart
and a tempest rages outside
set dissenting branches to break.
The darkened moon in distress weeps
to see us snatched away at night.

We could return to the old path
if our countrymen cast an eye
over the marred face of the land.
We can stop doing Cain's bidding
 and cast our hearts into pardon.

I would be as dull as an ass
that has swallowed selected gold
but made for its bassinet dust
if I do not embrace peace now
but not at any price of course.

The World's Nightmare

It cannot survive in pity
nor settle where laughter giggles.
It cannot reach to heaven
nor spare the sparkling of a star.
It does not care about treason
and stands in the way of all folks,
ready to give them fake freedom
and seal the fate of every heart.

It knows nothing about justice
nor democracy and suffrage.
The rich and the poor slake its thirst
and the stupid and the clever
bulge out its stomach everyday
but it is never satisfied.
The freedom to go anywhere
makes it make us objects of scorn.

Death neither sings nor celebrates
like man in glee or in deadlock.
It can only bite and blow out life
unseen, the nightmare of the world.
The world though insatiate hates you
and thanatophiles now and then
call in question your faithfulness.
I spit on you the world's nightmare.

When Innocence Is Slain

I grieve for you countrymen
from shadows of old palm trees.
The beast in the heart of greed,
the shine of all that is dung
and the lust so strong in man
make my head spin round and round
like a dead leaf from a branch.

Though your honesty lies slain
on the high grounds of power
far from the dreams of your youth,
though your dreams rot in the earth
trampled to death by foul feet
waiting in the wings to reign,
I keep the truth of your lives.
It will be scattered past fields
into the hearts of sound minds.

I grieve for you my brethren
from the ashes of your light
put out to pull down fairness.
I care not what experts say
for when innocence is slain
the heart loses its sparkle
and the mind goes on exile.

You Worry Too Much

You worry just too much mate
of what the other side says,
a circle of hounds and wolves.
I do not, I am pebble.

This is no time to fret friend
nor the place to take cover.
The crickets have all decamped
and the birds too have bolted
back to the place we caressed
gambolling in the green grass
as kids on their mothers' breasts.

If my hunger to quit drowns
and the impasse defies time
with the typhoon in my heart
making things worse everyday,
the hands of time will divulge
after reshaping our fate.
I do not need the favour
of souls wearing scorpion smiles.
This land belongs to us all,
seasons of shadows or not.

The Last Decent Soldier

Half-crazed, the soldier stood
near the trench he crawled out of
gazing at his dead mates
without really seeing them,
wondering what to do next,
the last decent soldier.
Death spat him out for now
but he did not understand
why he was not brought down
by enemy bombardment.
His heart pounded with blues
the last loyal soldier.

He sighed deeply and wept
knowing the fight was still on
as long as he had life.
He banished fear and weakness,
shot himself for his mates,
the last engaged fighter.
Love drove him to die too
near the trench teeming with flies.
As I stood there thinking
vultures swooped for a great meal.
He has spurred my spirit
this last sincere soldier,
this season of shadows.

Left In The Cold

The hitman in his twenties
lost both life and the honour
he fought to bring to the land.
Hearts clothed in smoky garments,
not knowing which way to turn
claim he gave in to suicide.
I cannot undress their claims
this season of crankiness.

Amidst raging tongues of hate
leaving wide open our wounds ,
I have given all I have
of the mind and of the heart
to stop the intense dislike
that could beget a bloodbath.
Sleep has left me in the cold,
shadows, blood in their eyes laugh.

The warrior battled for Love
to make a home in our hearts
and save the land from wilting.
He died in a needless war
for hoggish statesmen to rule
prying open thighs to live,
unaffected, remorseless
even this season of tears.

Strength Gone Not The Mind

My strength has shrunk, not my mind.
The chant of the spring near me
keeps my head at work all day.
The base behaviour of dons
shakes my frame like a whirlwind
in the heart of dry weather.
I have struggled to stifle
the stout urge of going back
where we were licked into shape
under the eyes of forebears,
eyes red like flames in a forge.
My head, my memory know this.

I hope you sing as we did
before plump dreams drove us here
where hearts as cold as chilled cheese
stand tall and dish out brain bugs.
Had I the culture of beasts
I would savage their culture.

My strength has shrunk, not my mind.
The hissing of the night wind
upsets my ears, not my mind
this season of psychosis.
I do not wish to wear gloom
even this goading season.

The Yoke That Burdens

Get all the fame,
get all the land
and feed Ambition to explode.
Get to the top of the mountain,
talk down to your own kith and kin
but do not forget Time's passage.

Grab all the riches,
grab all the headlines
and celebrate Sycophancy.
Grab all the chieftaincy titles,
grind the faces of your brethren
but remember that when you swim
far away from the shore, you drown.

Go to all places,
go to the moon too
and venerate Mediocrity,
the yoke that really burdens me.
The tribalism in your blood
and the heavy hand of your god
would lay waste this beautiful land,
this land of talent and manna.
The yoke that actually burdens
is your animus for the land.

The Heads Gone

Understand that the heads gone
though they were not scholastic,
their patriotism stood out
on top of all dark shadows.
Their ideas though lean like beef
and sometimes even tasteless
lacked nothing a good heart needs.

Swindling unlike the present
did not spread across the land.
Overweening pride and airs
though present never threatened.
The headmen of old had hearts
that beat for the common good.
Now that they are gone we sway
like an old hut in the wind.
I see a sea of mad flames
roar and consume the madness
that forces the heart to hide.
The heads gone remain icons.

Begotten Of Rogues

They put all under their feet
sniffing the snuff of power,
scoundrels begotten of rogues.
They tread in unmeasured steps
and vomit their recklessness
in the coldness of the night
before the homes of those marked
for the central sacrifice,
the sacrifice to save heads
that have betrayed you and I
in drunken bouts for the Duce.

Many have sunk in their blood
or succumbed on the scaffold.
Many have been tossed away
like bedraggled overlays,
humiliated and ground down.
The moon's eyes are dim with grief,
the call of trees in the night
and night birds that drop their tears
on the breasts of Mother Earth,
bid us sing songs with handcuffs.
Il Duce must be caged or hanged.

They Expect A Fee

Succubus lurks in the streets.
Those who fall for her sing rhymes.
Some sly calamitous fleets
of drunks and suspicious climes
storm the byways like locusts,
spreading slogans not focused.

Strange spears hurtle before me
and unknown voices scoff too.
They expect a fee from me
to drink from their dirty trough.
I have the right to let fly
in the deep, your call to spy.
If you sway your consciences
my leech landsmen to survey
the mercy killing warrants
you carry, you will hot tears
convey to the world outside.
Betrayal has its downside.

In anger I shut my door
to stir to life dying flames
and make crystalline the floor
where we can new frames put up
in mockery of the aged forms
towering us without norms.

You Dare Not Be Silent

I wish my thoughts were termites
and my mouth a burning mount,
I will consume all turnpikes
and smoke each shadowy mind.
I think it better to burn
in times like these, the mind's muck.
You dare not be indifferent.

I wish I grew in your heart
and raised a monument there,
I will chart a new outlet
and make dark consciences flare.
Patriots dare not be silent
when fifth columns grow violent
and our dignity drops tears.

I sing the dirge day and night
for the murder of wordsmiths
who could have shamed sway and might
in seasons of threats and blood.
You dare not be silent friend
when a new terror is born.
My heart is filled this season,
season of fustian shadows
with an unspeakable dread.

Likely Tempest

The air is heavy with foulness
and naked children with dry mouths
gaze in fear a likely tempest.
Surely indoors orphans tremble
amid growing fears of long sleep.
Cockroaches lick the last cheap oil
glistening on wretched bodies
worn out by hard work without gain,
this sickening season of doubt.

Toadies taunt these plain souls with slime,
rubbing their valued traditions
with cowpat before tearing them.
Sometimes my rage reddens unchecked
in the album of my stay here
dodging the sledge hammer of hate
and drinking the bitter waters
in the camp of the knocked about.
Sometimes I tiptoe to the gorge
where they are tossed away when dead,
holding firmly my dissent heart
lest I be provoked to hatred.

Burn Your Rags

When our way is full of thorns,
when our food is but endless thoughts
and we think the end has come,
the owner of life picks us up,
dusts us if we desire
and weaves a garland round our necks
to burn the rags of our pain
in a system without brains.

When our roots are tampered with,
when the heart of our life is sore
and we feel serpents have won,
the owner of life draws us near,
gives us milk if we need it
and weaves a big basket for us
to heave food to the hungry
in a state that hates laundry.

When the heart is filled with grief,
when our birthright stands in the cold
and vultures step in to sing,
the owner of the world meets us,
gives us words and material
to break the barriers round us
and hoist the flag of freedom
in a land that loves thraldom.

Still My Heart

Cast a slur my countrymen
upon the shameless shadows
showering us with shingles
that leave patches on our skins,
beasts bleeding the nation dry.
Drain to the dregs my people
the milk that moves the bowels
this season of sophistry.

Cast stabbing stones my kinsmen
upon the Devil's frontmen
holding fast to our holdings,
awaiting the fall of foes.
Your gesture will still my heart
still bleeding from defilement.
Let the hearts of hurting souls
find hearth and home in your hearts.

May this season of shadows
as treacherous as the sea
bring you face to face with facts
to clean the land so so stained.
Still my heart kinsmen when souls
wait in dung with bated breath
the budding of better days.

Printed in the United States
By Bookmasters